Treasury of Patchwork Borders

Full-Size Patterns for 76 Designs

BY

ELIZABETH F. NYHAN

DOVER PUBLICATIONS, INC.
New York

Copyright © 1991 by Elizabeth F. Nyhan.
All rights reserved under Pan American and International Copyright Conventions.

Published in Canada by General Publishing Company, Ltd., 30 Lesmill Road, Don Mills, Toronto, Ontario.
Published in the United Kingdom by Constable and Company, Ltd., 3 The Lanchesters, 162–164 Fulham Palace Road, London W6 9ER.

Treasury of Patchwork Borders: Full-Size Patterns for 76 Designs is a new work, first published by Dover Publications, Inc., in 1991.

Manufactured in the United States of America
Dover Publications, Inc., 31 East 2nd Street, Mineola, N.Y. 11501

Library of Congress Cataloging-in-Publication Data

Nyhan, Elizabeth F.
    Treasury of patchwork borders : full-size patterns for 76 designs / by Elizabeth F. Nyhan.
        p.   cm. — (Dover needlework series)
    ISBN 0-486-26183-2 (pbk.)
    1. Patchwork—Patterns.   I. Title.   II. Series.
TT835.N94   1991
746.9′7041—dc20   90-47192
                                                                              CIP

INTRODUCTION

Just as a photograph or painting is set off by a well-chosen frame, so is a quilt enhanced by a well-designed border. A quilt with no border seems incomplete somehow, while one with a poorly designed border looks amateurish. Given two quilts in competition, both with the same main design and the same quality of workmanship, the one with a well-planned border would probably win.

The simplest border consists of plain strips of fabric. This simple border should not be underrated. It is very effective when used to divide multiple border patterns *(Fig. 1)*, as a dividing strip between quilt blocks *(Fig. 2)* or as the outer edge of the quilt *(Fig. 3)*. Using several rows of strips in different fabrics and widths can also make an attractive border *(Fig. 4)*.

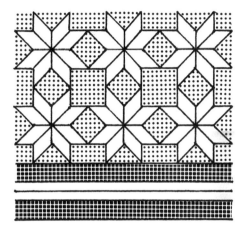

FIGURE 3

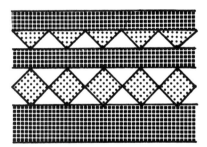

FIGURE 1

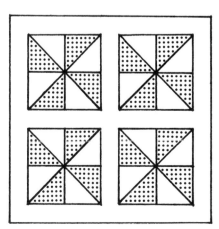

FIGURE 2

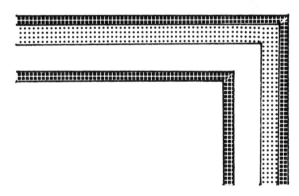

FIGURE 4

For those who want to go beyond this simple, plain border, the patchwork border opens up new areas of design possibilities. A patchwork border can complement and accent the design of a patchwork quilt and can add drama and excitement to a whole-cloth quilt. This book offers 76 different patchwork borders for you to choose from.

All of the borders in this book are placed in the middle of a plain background in order to show the design clearly. Alternatively, the border can be sewn right next to another border strip or to the main body of the quilt. This can give the design a completely different character *(Fig. 5)*.

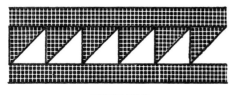

FIGURE 5

A specific rule cannot be stated for determining the width of a border. If the quilt is composed of repeating blocks, a border the same width or slightly larger than the block size is a good starting place. Not all quilts feature a block design, however, so you must use your own judgment. In addition, if the quilt must be a specific size to fit on a bed, the border must be planned accordingly.

A good, although not inflexible, principle to follow in designing a border is to choose design elements similar in type and size to those found in the main body of the quilt. For example, a border with diamonds is a better choice for a Lone Star quilt than one with rectangles. If you want to use pieces of a different size than those in the body of the quilt, make them smaller rather than larger.

Although great thought may be given to the planning of the main body of a quilt, the border is often an afterthought. If you want to experiment with patchwork borders, for best results plan the border at the same time as the rest of the quilt.

The design of the corner, which is often taken for granted when looking at the finished product, presents a challenge even to an accomplished quilter. For this reason, a corner has been created for each border in this book. Sometimes a pattern will be shown with several different corners. Wherever possible, background and corner pieces should be mitered for a more professional look.

Each of the borders shown can be made in five different sizes, using the full-size patterns given on pages 55–63 of this book. Each border is shown on a grid, where one square equals one square "unit." This unit can measure 1″, 1½″, 2″, 2½″ or 3″. For example, pattern piece N measures two units square. If the unit measurement is 1″, piece N is 2″ square; if the unit measurement is 3″, piece N is 6″ square. All five sizes of each pattern piece are shown together, one inside the other, with each one marked with the unit size. To use the patterns, trace the desired size onto translucent plastic or onto paper. Glue the paper to lightweight cardboard. In order to avoid confusion, seam allowances have *not* been added to the pieces, so, if you are planning to sew the pieces together by machine, add ¼″ around each piece now. If you are planning to sew the

pieces together by hand, it is not necessary to add the seam allowance to the templates. Cut out the templates.

Each border design is shown as if it were the bottom half of a quilt. The main design of the border, called the *repeat section*, which occurs over and over, is marked; the border width is also marked. All possible centers are marked. Usually the center occurs at the middle or at the end of a repeat section *(Fig. 6)*. A chart is included which

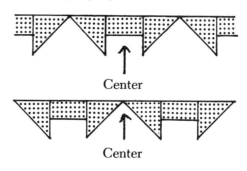

FIGURE 6

lists the actual measurements in inches of the repeat section and the border width for the five different sets of pattern pieces. A piecing diagram for the repeat section is shown along with separate diagrams of the pattern pieces required. If more than one piecing method is possible, the optional method(s) and pattern pieces are shown. If special piecing is needed for the corner, this is shown along with the extra pattern pieces required. Sometimes a choice of several corner treatments is shown.

Often a border with a particular repeat section can be rearranged to form a totally different border. For example, the border might be facing inside instead of outside, the center may be handled differently, or some of the repeat section pieces may be turned differently. These variations are shown after the main border design. Since the repeat section and border width are the same as for the main border design, separate size charts and piecing diagrams are not given.

To begin designing your border, first draw the quilt to scale on graph paper. At least half of the quilt should be drawn. This way, problems such as border width, the use of improper design elements or the need for plain border strips become very obvious.

Choose the border pattern you want to use, then decide what size pieces work best with the main body of the quilt. Choose the unit size based on that decision. Suppose you want to use Border 1, and you would like to use triangles that measure 3″ on each short side. As you see from the border diagram, the short side of each triangle in this design is two units long. Divide 3″ by 2 units to get the unit size of 1½″.

If the border you have chosen has more than one center, you must now decide which one to use. Starting at the center, draw the design out to the corner showing both possibilities. Sometimes the handling of the corner will dictate which center should be used. In *Fig. 7*, the repeat section fits exactly and one of the corner variations can be used. In *Fig. 8*, the center has been shifted. A problem occurs at the corner. The design is symmetrical, but not as pleasing to the eye as the one in *Fig. 7*.

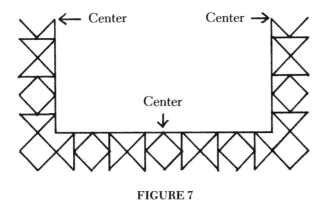

FIGURE 7

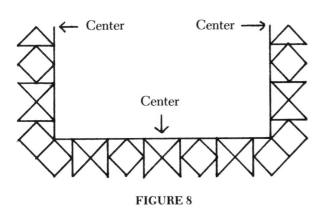

FIGURE 8

In some cases, the repeat patterns will not come out evenly and none of the suggested corners will work. If this happens, you can adjust the size of the quilt by adding plain border strips; you can design an alternative border; or you can choose a different border pattern.

Work with your drawing until you have a border and corner treatment you are happy with. It is much easier to deal with problems on paper than to discover them after the quilt top has been sewn together. Once you have your border on paper, you can begin to sew.

When the center of your quilt is complete, press it carefully, then measure each side to make sure that opposite sides are the same length. If necessary, adjust the seamlines. If the quilt measurements have changed since you made your sketch, adjust the drawing before cutting the pieces for the border. Mark the center of each side of the quilt.

First cut and sew any plain border strips to the quilt. Cut these strips the length of the side, plus twice the cut width of the strip, plus 2". For a 3"-wide border on a 66"-long side, cut the strip 3½" × 75". Pin the border strips to the quilt with the ends extending evenly. Stitch, beginning and ending the stitching ¼" from the corners of the quilt. With the quilt top right side up, turn under the top border strip on each corner so that a 45° angle is formed from the inner corner of the border to the outer corner. Press the fold. Bring the edges of the quilt together with the right sides in and stitch the borders together, using the crease as a guide. Trim the excess.

Referring to your drawing, determine how many of each piece you will need for your patchwork border. Trace the templates to the wrong side of the fabric, being sure to allow room for seam allowances on pieces for hand sewing. Some asymmetrical templates may need to be reversed before tracing, so check your drawing carefully. Cut out the pieces. When cutting out pieces for hand sewing, be sure to cut ¼" outside of the traced line.

Sew all pieces with right sides together. For hand sewing, match the traced seamlines, and sew exactly on the line, starting and stopping exactly on the ends of the line. For machine sewing, use the cut edge of the fabric as a guide for the presser foot. Press all seams to one side.

When the border is complete and sewn to the center of the quilt top, assemble the quilt top, batting and backing. Quilt as desired, then bind the edges.

BORDER 1

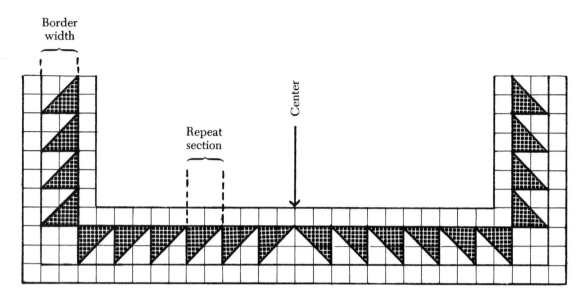

UNIT MEASUREMENT	1″	1½″	2″	2¼″	3″
Repeat section width	2″	3″	4″	5″	6″
Border width	2″	3″	4″	5″	6″

REPEAT SECTION PIECING	PIECES REQUIRED	EXTRA PIECES REQUIRED FOR CORNER
	E	K

Variation 1

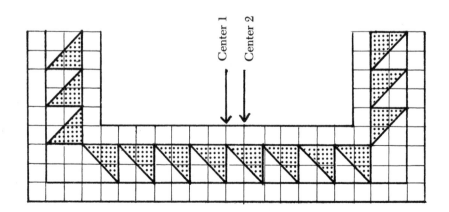

Variation 2

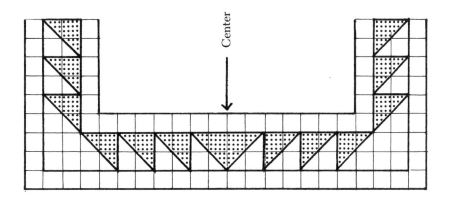

Variation 3

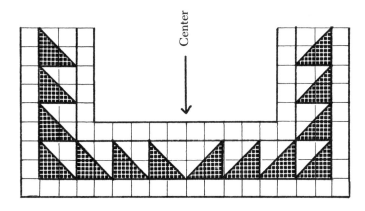

Variation 4

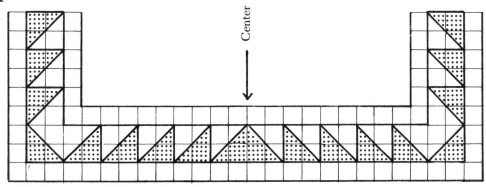

Variation 5

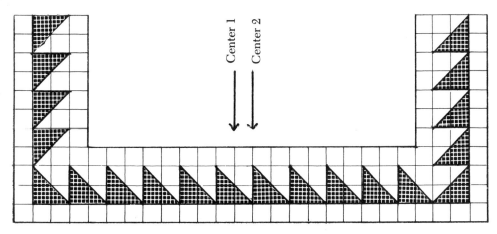

BORDER 2

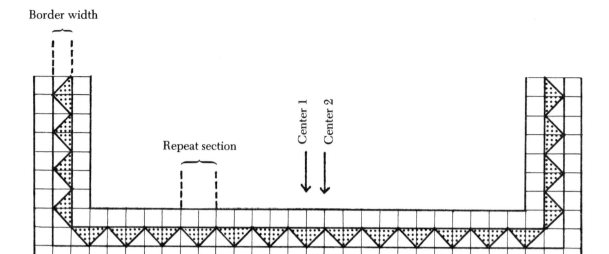

Unit Measurement	1″	1½″	2″	2½″	3″
Repeat section width	2″	3″	4″	5″	6″
Border width	1″	1½″	2″	2½″	3″

REPEAT SECTION PIECING

1.

2.

PIECES REQUIRED

C

C   A

Variation 1

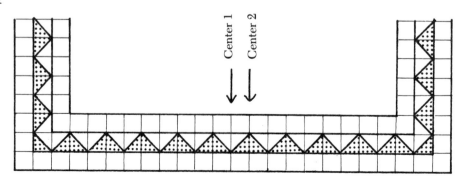

BORDER 3

Border width

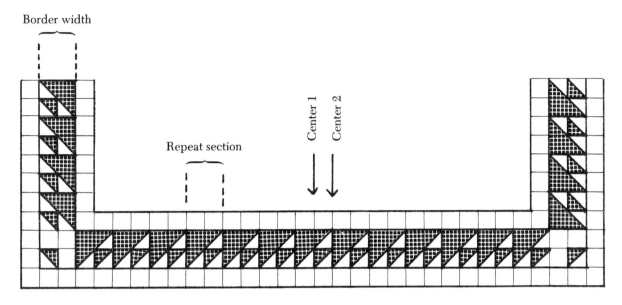

Repeat section

Center 1 Center 2

Unit Measurement	1″	1½″	2″	2½″	3″
Repeat section width	2″	3″	4″	5″	6″
Border width	2″	3″	4″	5″	6″

REPEAT SECTION PIECING	PIECES REQUIRED	CORNER PIECING	EXTRA PIECES REQUIRED

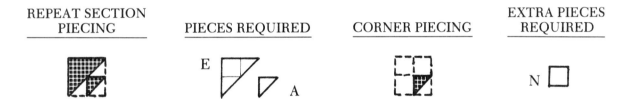

E   A   N

Variation 1

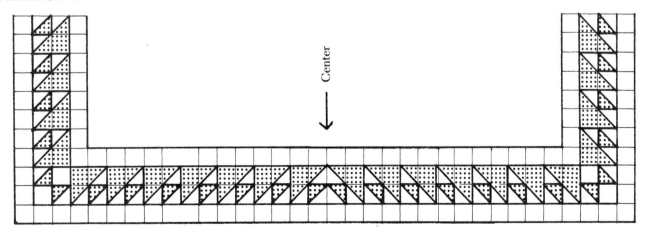

Center

CORNER PIECING

Variation 2

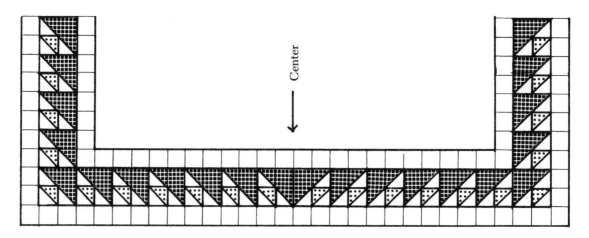

Variation 3

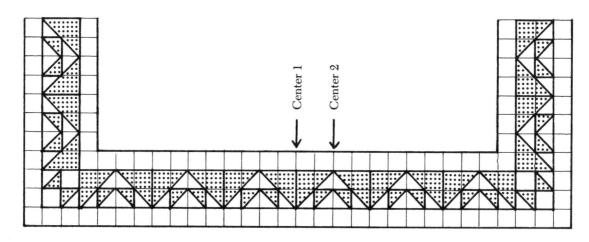

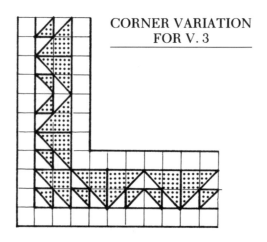

CORNER VARIATION
FOR V. 3

Variation 4—*same as V. 1, but facing inward*

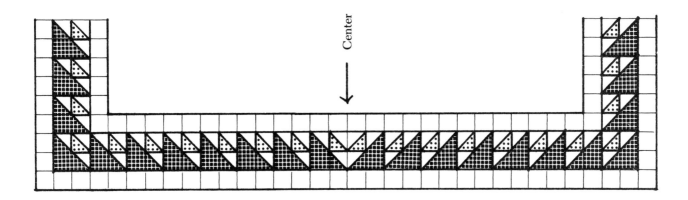

Variation 5—*same as V. 2, but facing inward*

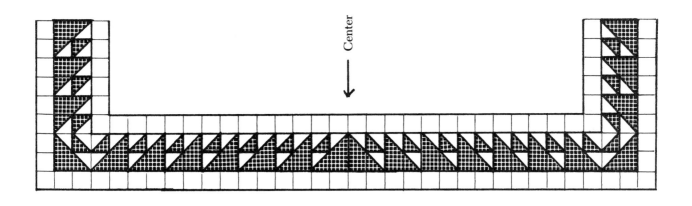

Variation 6—*same as V. 3, but facing inward*

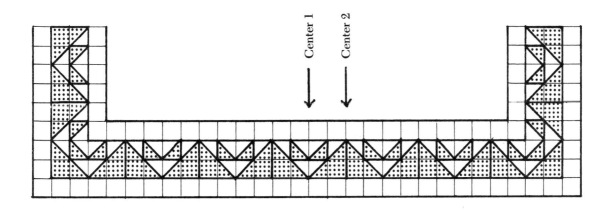

BORDER 4

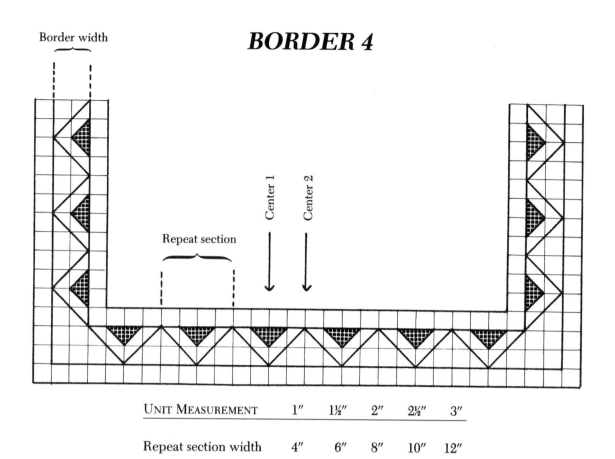

Border width

Center 1
Center 2

Repeat section

Unit Measurement	1″	1½″	2″	2½″	3″
Repeat section width	4″	6″	8″	10″	12″
Border width	2″	3″	4″	5″	6″

REPEAT SECTION PIECING

PIECES REQUIRED

A   F   E

CORNER PIECING

Variation 1

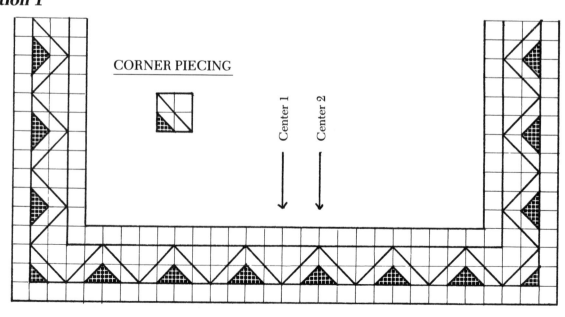

CORNER PIECING

Center 1
Center 2

BORDER 5

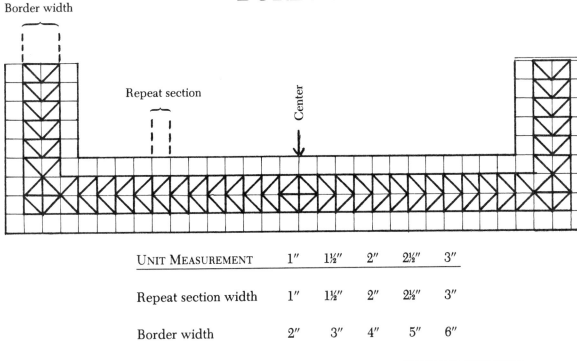

UNIT MEASUREMENT	1″	1½″	2″	2½″	3″
Repeat section width	1″	1½″	2″	2½″	3″
Border width	2″	3″	4″	5″	6″

REPEAT SECTION PIECING	PIECES REQUIRED	CORNER/CENTER PIECING

Variation 1—*same as original design, except that the triangles point toward the center*

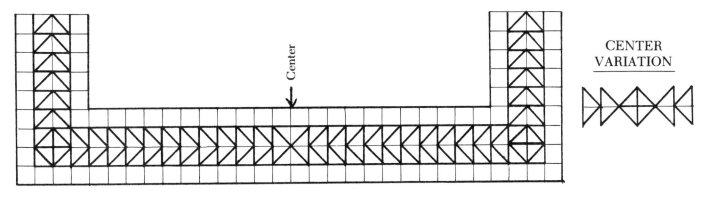

Variation 2—*all triangles pointing in the same direction*

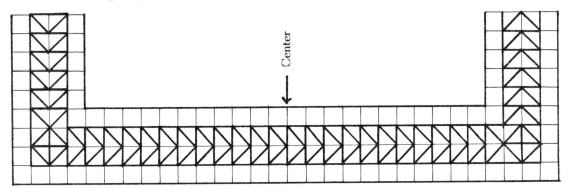

BORDER 6

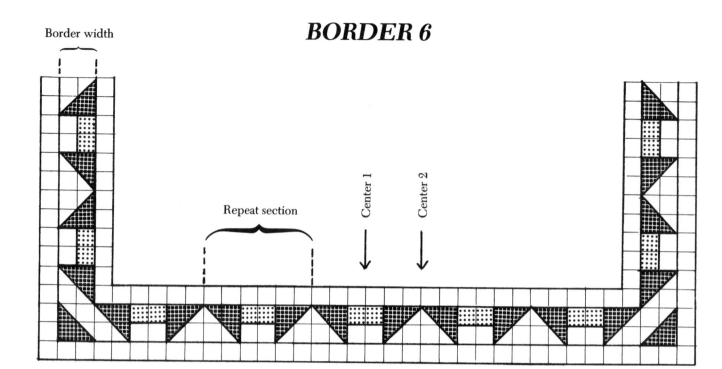

Unit Measurement	1″	1½″	2″	2½″	3″
Repeat section width	6″	9″	12″	15″	18″
Border width	2″	3″	4″	5″	6″

REPEAT SECTION PIECING

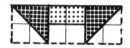

PIECES REQUIRED

 E   J

CORNER PIECING

Variation 1—*same design, facing inward*

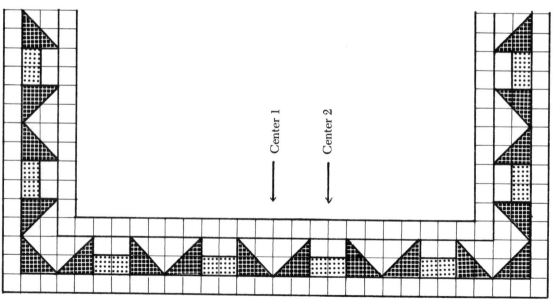

14

BORDER 7

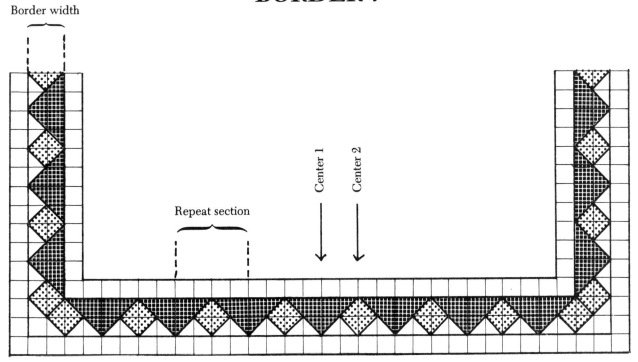

Border width

Repeat section

Center 1 Center 2

UNIT MEASUREMENT	1″	1½″	2″	2½″	3″
Repeat section width	4″	6″	8″	10″	12″
Border width	2″	3″	4″	5″	6″

REPEAT SECTION PIECING

PIECES REQUIRED

E   B   C

CORNER PIECING

Variation 1—*same design, facing inward*

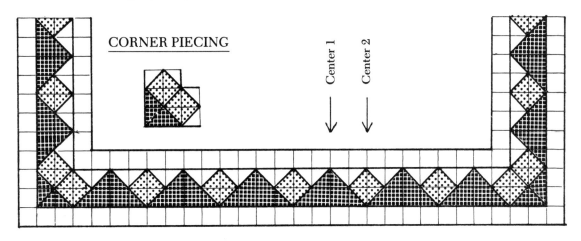

CORNER PIECING

Center 1   Center 2

BORDER 8

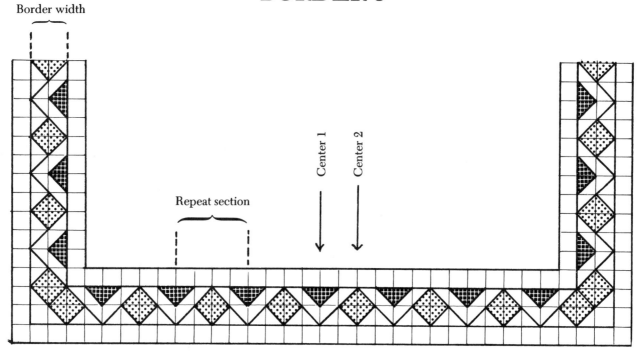

Unit Measurement	1″	1½″	2″	2½″	3″
Repeat section width	4″	6″	8″	10″	12″
Border width	2″	3″	4″	5″	6″

REPEAT SECTION PIECING

PIECES REQUIRED

Variation 1—*same design, facing inward*

CORNER VARIATION

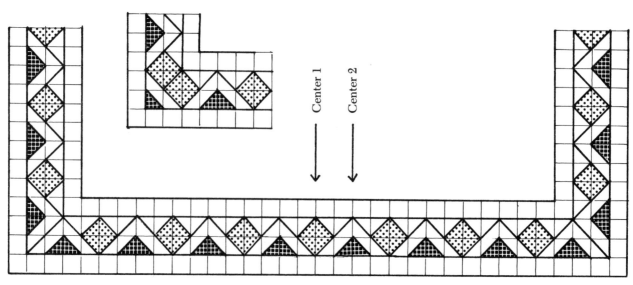

BORDER 9

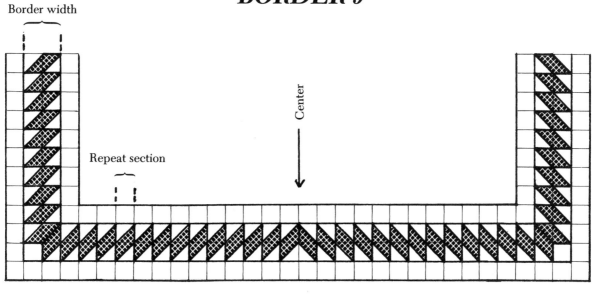

Border width

Center

Repeat section

UNIT MEASUREMENT	1″	1½″	2″	2½″	3″
Repeat section width	1″	1½″	2″	2½″	3″
Border width	2″	3″	4″	5″	6″

REPEAT SECTION PIECING	PIECES REQUIRED	CORNER PIECING	EXTRA PIECES REQUIRED
	P ⟋ ◺ A		N □

Variation 1

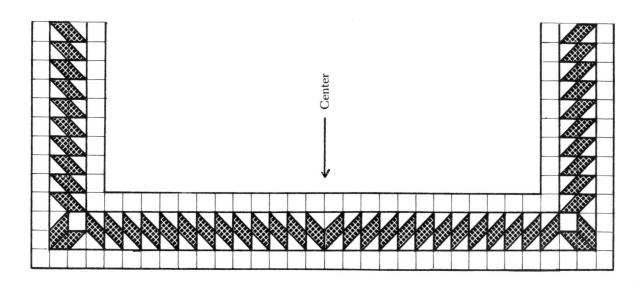

Center

BORDER 10

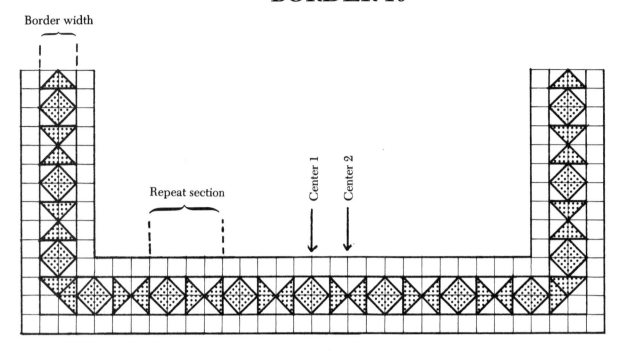

Border width

Repeat section

Center 1 Center 2

Unit Measurement	1″	1½″	2″	2½″	3″
Repeat section width	4″	6″	8″	10″	12″
Border width	2″	3″	4″	5″	6″

REPEAT SECTION PIECING

1.

2.

3.

PIECES REQUIRED

B · A · C

A · C

A · C

CORNER PIECING

CORNER VARIATIONS

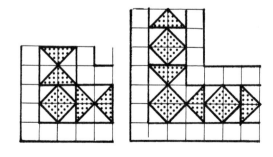

Variation 1—*same piecing as main design, but in the squares with the four triangles, the pattern and background fabrics are reversed*

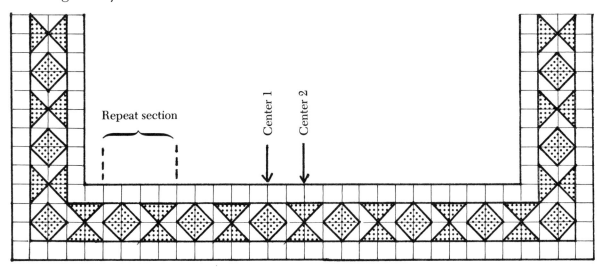

BORDER 11

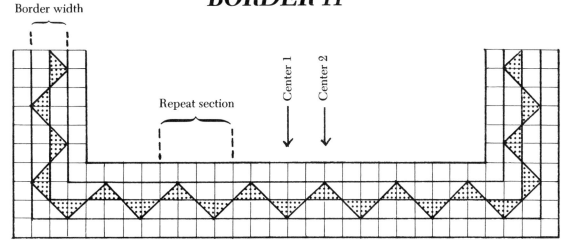

Unit Measurement	1″	1½″	2″	2½″	3″
Repeat section width	4″	6″	8″	10″	12″
Border width	2″	3″	4″	5″	6″

REPEAT SECTION PIECING	PIECES REQUIRED	CORNER PIECING
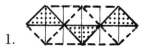 1. 2. 	 	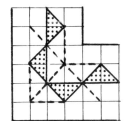

19

BORDER 12

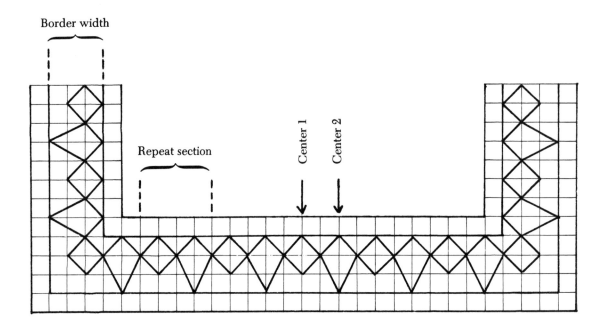

Border width

Repeat section

Center 1

Center 2

Unit Measurement	1″	1½″	2″	2½″	3″
Repeat section width	4″	6″	8″	10″	12″
Border width	3″	4½″	6″	7½″	9″

REPEAT SECTION PIECING

1.

2.

3.

PIECES REQUIRED

A M H G
C

A C G
M O

A
M G

CORNER PIECING

EXTRA PIECES REQUIRED

I

Variation 1—*same design, facing inward*

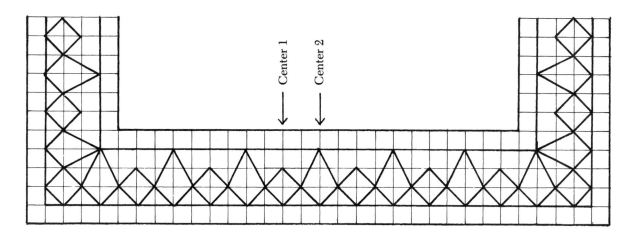

CORNER PIECING   PIECES REQUIRED

BORDER 13

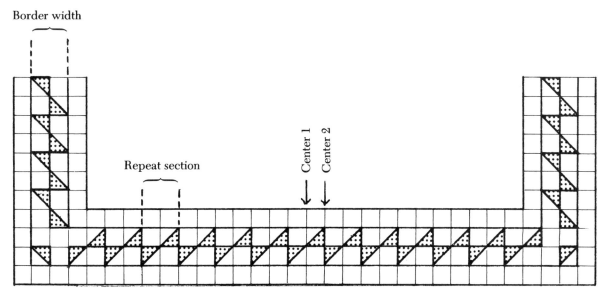

Unit Measurement	1″	1½″	2″	2½″	3″
Repeat section width	2″	3″	4″	5″	6″
Border width	2″	3″	4″	5″	6″

REPEAT SECTION PIECING

PIECES REQUIRED

N   A

CORNER PIECING

BORDER 14

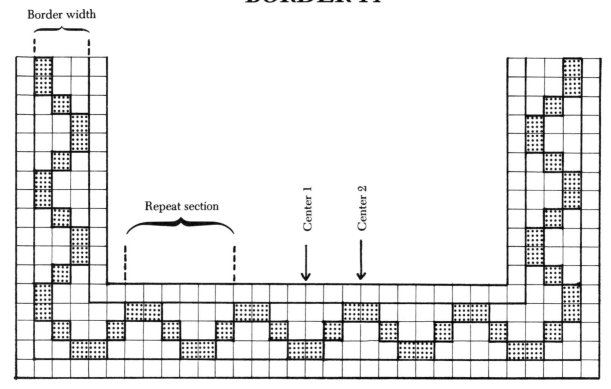

Border width

Repeat section

Center 1

Center 2

Unit Measurement	1″	1½″	2″	2½″	3″
Repeat section width	6″	9″	12″	15″	18″
Border width	3″	4½″	6″	7½″	9″

REPEAT SECTION PIECING

PIECES REQUIRED

J K N

CORNER PIECING

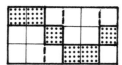
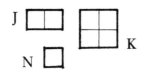

CORNER VARIATION

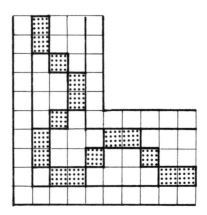

BORDER 15

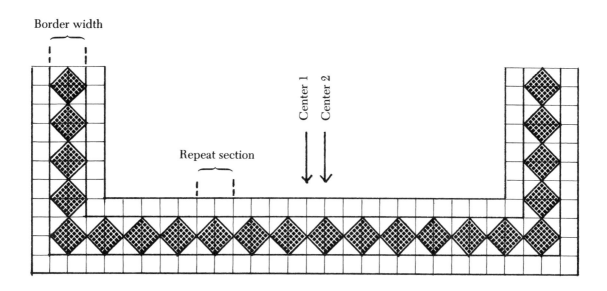

Unit Measurement	1″	1½″	2″	2½″	3″
Repeat section width	2″	3″	4″	5″	6″
Border width	2″	3″	4″	5″	6″

REPEAT SECTION PIECING

PIECES REQUIRED

1.

2.

3.

4.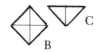

BORDER 16

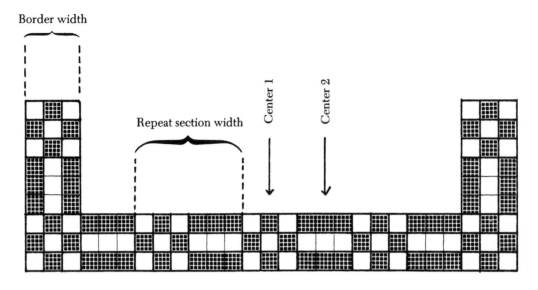

Border width

Repeat section width

Center 1

Center 2

Unit Measurement	1″	1½″	2″	2½″	3″
Repeat section width	6″	9″	12″	15″	18″
Border width	3″	4½″	6″	7½″	9″

REPEAT SECTION PIECING

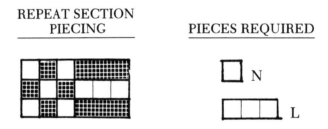

PIECES REQUIRED

N

L

Variation 1—*The length of the long strip between the checkerboards may be changed. The width of the repeat section depends on the length of this strip.*

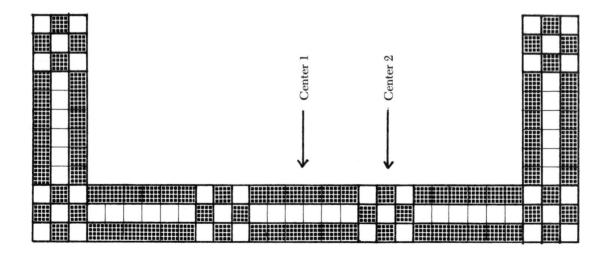

Center 1

Center 2

Variation 2—*The checkerboard may be enlarged to any size.*

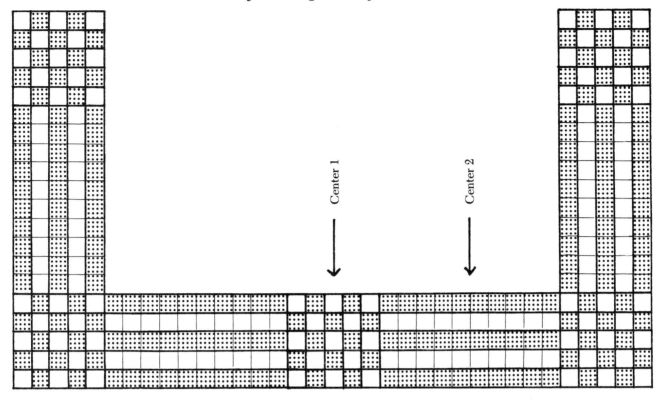

BORDER 17

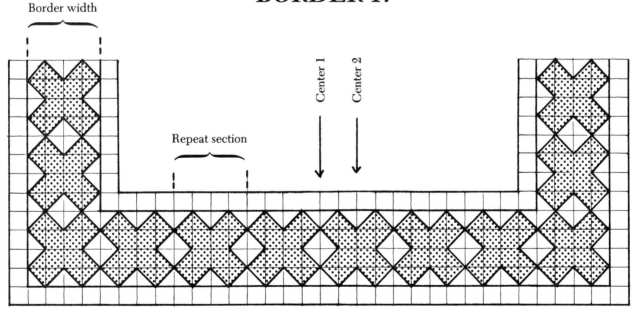

Unit Measurement	1″	1½″	2″	2½″	3″
Repeat section width	4″	6″	8″	10″	12″
Border width	4″	6″	8″	10″	12″

REPEAT SECTION PIECING

PIECES REQUIRED

BORDER 18

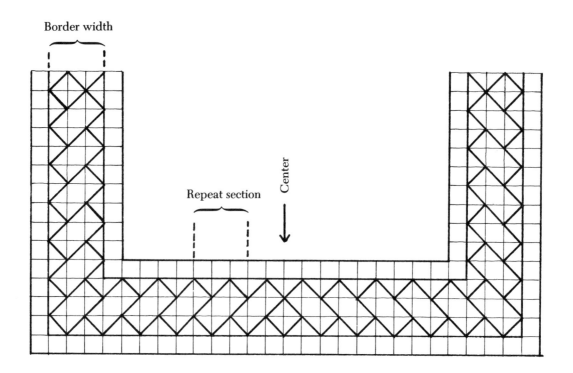

Border width

Repeat section

Center

Unit Measurement	1″	1½″	2″	2½″	3″
Repeat section width	3″	4½″	6″	7½″	9″
Border width	3″	4½″	6″	7½″	9″

REPEAT SECTION PIECING

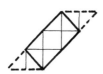

PIECES REQUIRED

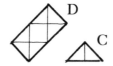

CENTER PIECING

EXTRA PIECES REQUIRED

CORNER PIECING

EXTRA PIECES REQUIRED

26

Variation 1

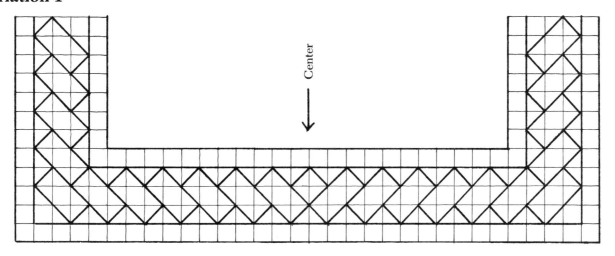

CORNER PIECING

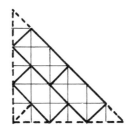

Variation 2

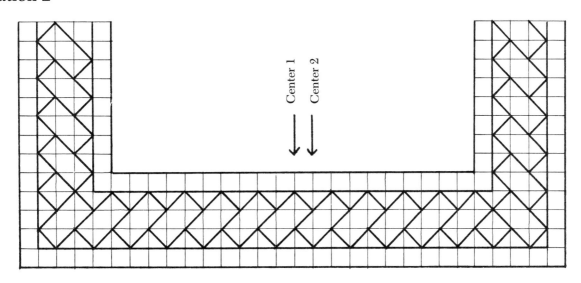

CORNER PIECING

EXTRA PIECES
REQUIRED

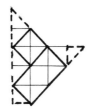

BORDER 19

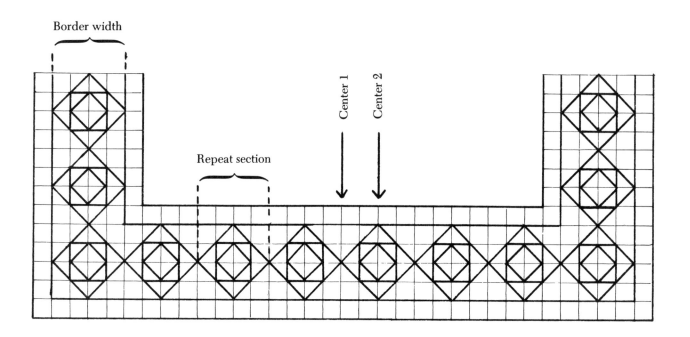

Unit Measurement	1″	1½″	2″	2½″	3″
Repeat section width	4″	6″	8″	10″	12″
Border width	4″	6″	8″	10″	12″

REPEAT SECTION PIECING

PIECES REQUIRED

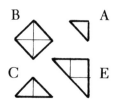

BORDER 20

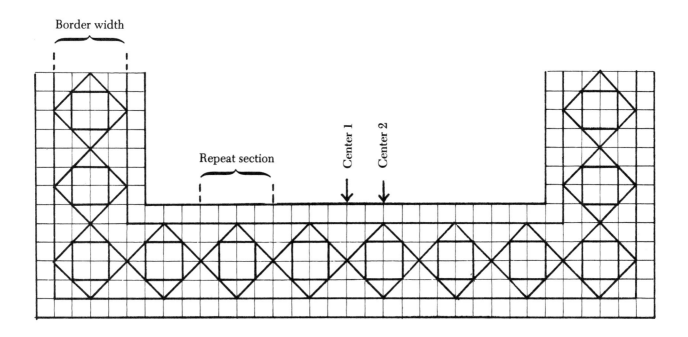

Unit Measurement	1″	1½″	2″	2½″	3″
Repeat section width	4″	6″	8″	10″	12″
Border width	4″	6″	8″	10″	12″

REPEAT SECTION
PIECING

PIECES REQUIRED

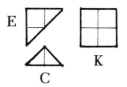

BORDER 21

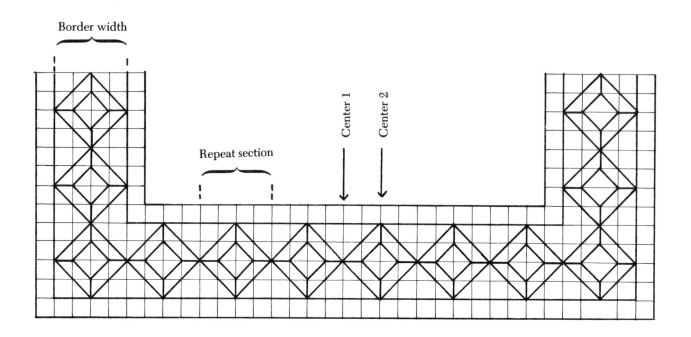

Unit Measurement	1″	1½″	2″	2½″	3″
Repeat section width	4″	6″	8″	10″	12″
Border width	4″	6″	8″	10″	12″

REPEAT SECTION PIECING

PIECES REQUIRED

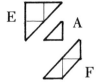

BORDER 22

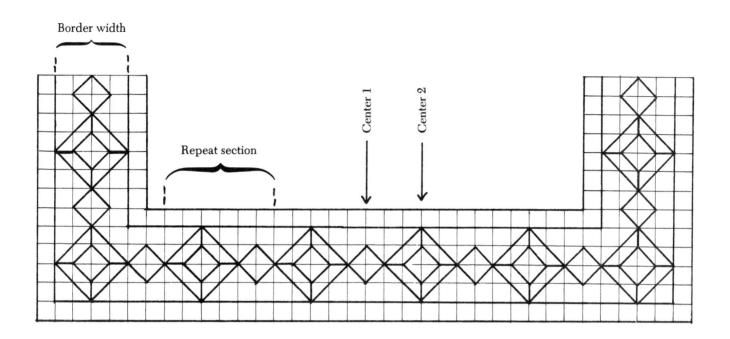

Border width

Repeat section

Center 1

Center 2

Unit Measurement	1″	1½″	2″	2½″	3″
Repeat section width	6″	9″	12″	15″	18″
Border width	4″	6″	8″	10″	12″

REPEAT SECTION PIECING

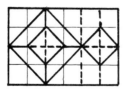

PIECES REQUIRED

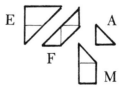

BORDER 23

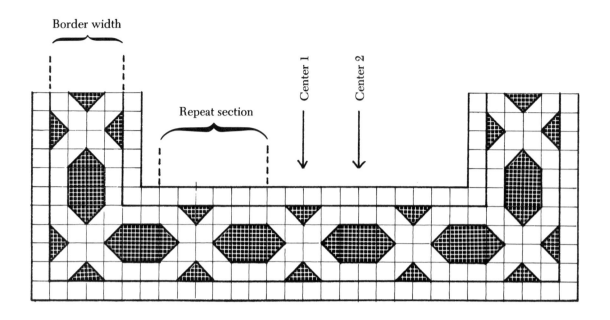

Unit Measurement	1″	1½″	2″	2½″	3″
Repeat section width	6″	9″	12″	15″	18″
Border width	4″	6″	8″	10″	12″

REPEAT SECTION PIECING

PIECES REQUIRED

1.
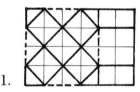
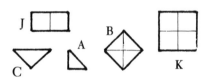

2.
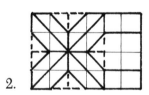
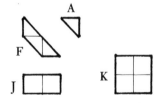

3.
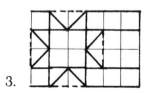
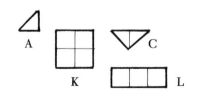

Variation 1—*different length between crosses*

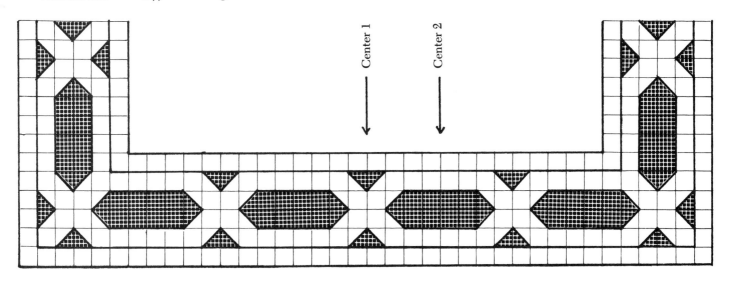

BORDER 24

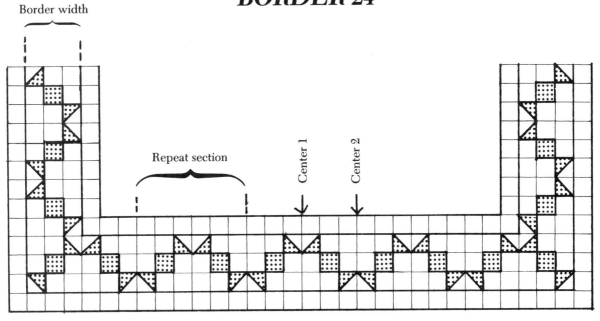

Unit Measurement	1″	1½″	2″	2½″	3″
Repeat section width	6″	9″	12″	15″	18″
Border width	3″	4½″	6″	7½″	9″

REPEAT SECTION PIECING

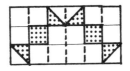

PIECES REQUIRED

BORDER 25

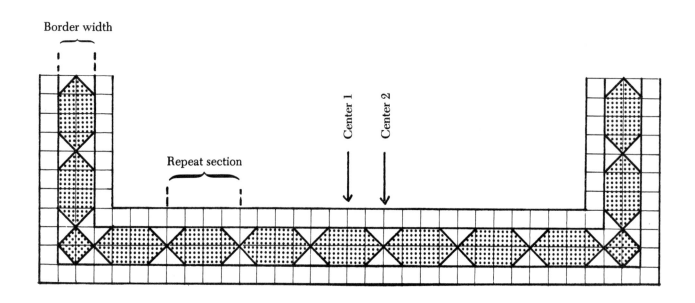

Border width

Repeat section

Center 1
Center 2

Unit Measurement	1″	1½″	2″	2½″	3″
Repeat section width	4″	6″	8″	10″	12″
Border width	2″	3″	4″	5″	6″

REPEAT SECTION PIECING

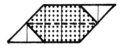

PIECES REQUIRED

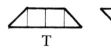

T   C

CORNER PIECING

EXTRA PIECES REQUIRED

A

BORDER 26

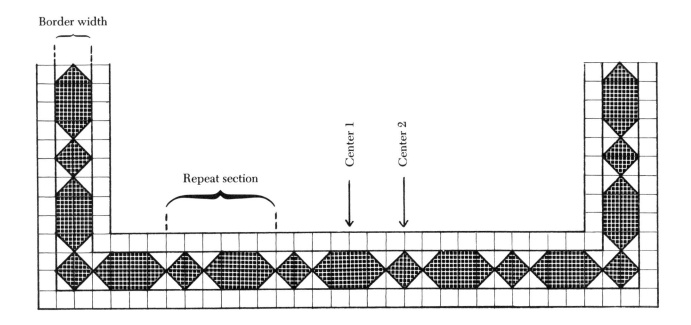

Border width

Repeat section

Center 1

Center 2

Unit Measurement	1″	1½″	2″	2½″	3″
Repeat section width	6″	9″	12″	15″	18″
Border width	2″	3″	4″	5″	6″

REPEAT SECTION PIECING

1.

2.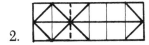

PIECES REQUIRED

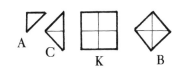

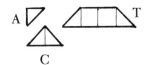

BORDER 27

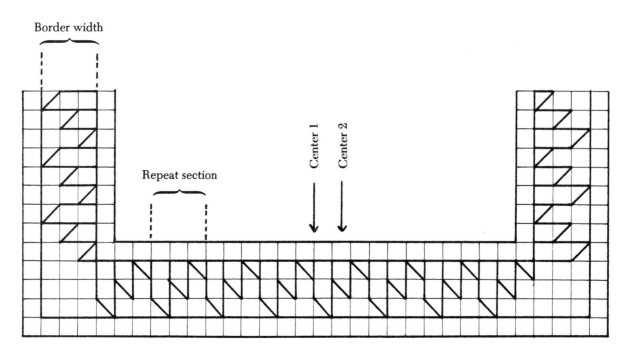

Border width

Repeat section

Center 1   Center 2

Unit Measurement	1″	1½″	2″	2¼″	3″
Repeat section width	3″	4½″	6″	7½″	9″
Border width	3″	4½″	6″	7½″	9″

REPEAT SECTION PIECING

PIECES REQUIRED

I   A

         M

CORNER PIECING

EXTRA PIECES REQUIRED

Block,
three units
square

Variation 1

Center

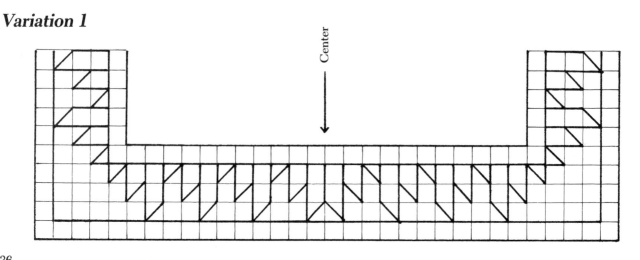

Variation 2

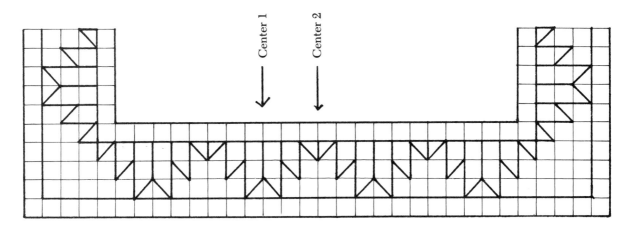

Variation 3—*same as V. 2, facing inward*

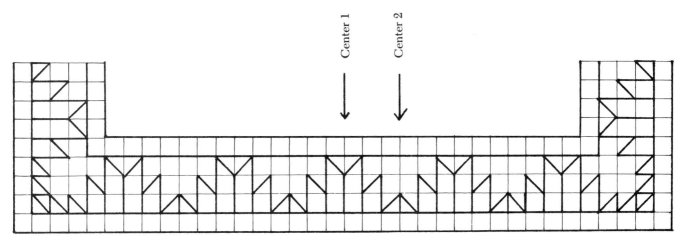

Variation 4—*using only two shapes from original design. This makes the repeat section one unit narrower.*

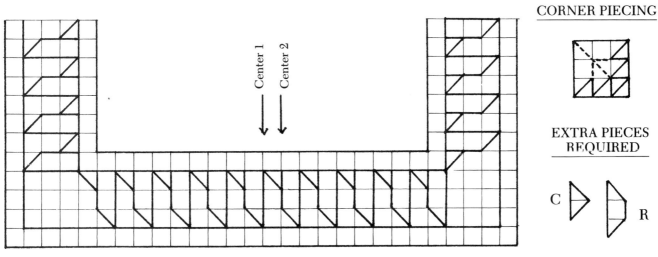

CORNER PIECING

EXTRA PIECES REQUIRED

C   R

Variation 5—*same as V. 4, facing inward*

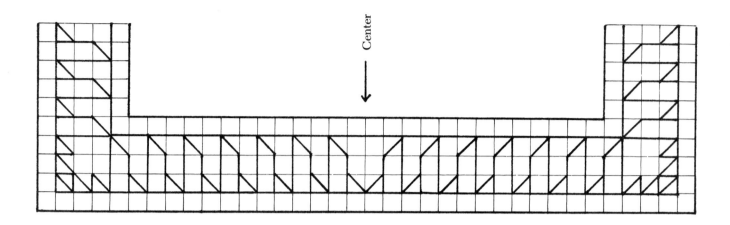

Variation 6—*original design pieces combined in decreasing height toward the corners*

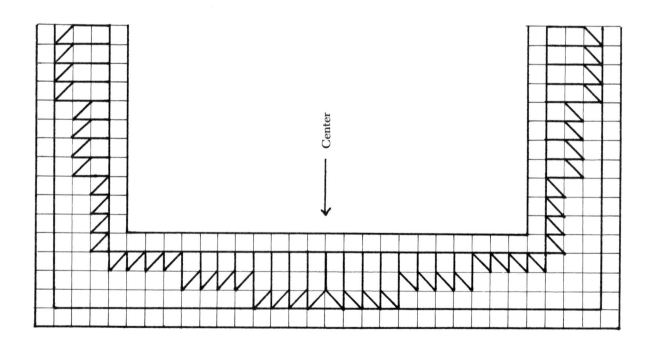

Variation 7—*same as V. 6, facing inward*

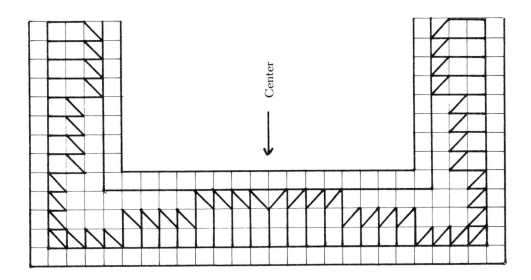

Variation 8—*same as V. 1, facing inward*

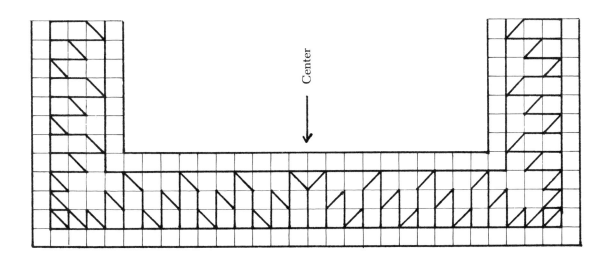

BORDER 28

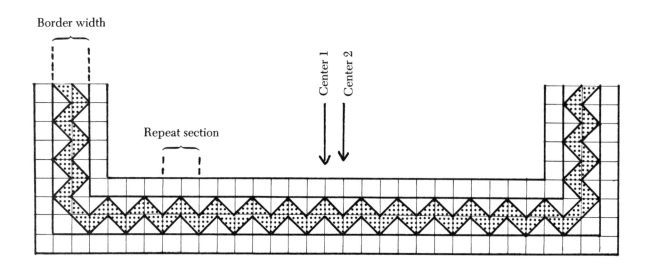

Unit Measurement	1″	1½″	2″	2½″	3″
Repeat section width	2″	3″	4″	5″	6″
Border width	2″	3″	4″	5″	6″

REPEAT SECTION PIECING

PIECES REQUIRED

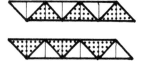

 C

Make and join
two strips
as shown

CORNER PIECING

EXTRA PIECES REQUIRED

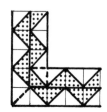

A

Variation 1—*increasing the number of strips*

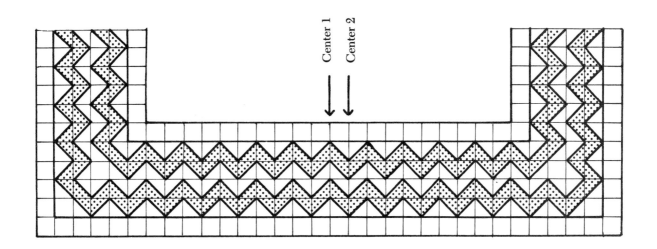

CORNER PIECING

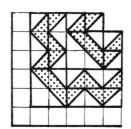

EXTRA PIECES REQUIRED

CORNER VARIATION

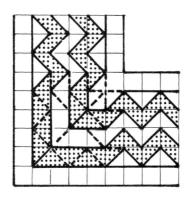

EXTRA PIECES REQUIRED

BORDER 29

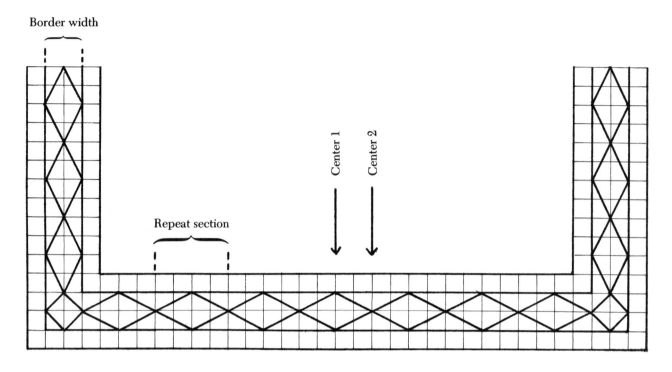

Border width

Center 1

Center 2

Repeat section

Unit Measurement	1″	1½″	2″	2½″	3″
Repeat section width	4″	6″	8″	10″	12″
Border width	2″	3″	4″	5″	6″

REPEAT SECTION PIECING

1.

2.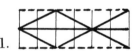

3.

PIECES REQUIRED

S

O
G

G

CORNER PIECING

1.

2.

CORNER VARIATION

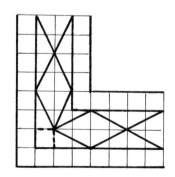

EXTRA PIECES REQUIRED

A
B

A

EXTRA PIECES REQUIRED

N
Q

BORDER 30

Border width

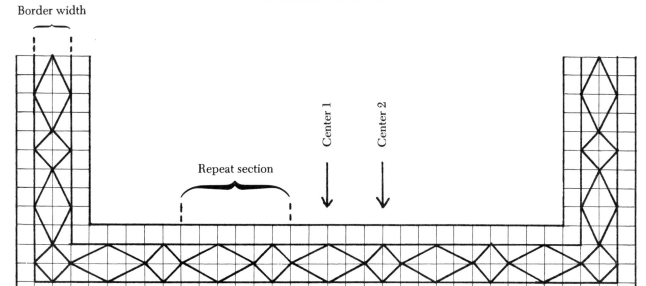

Repeat section

Center 1

Center 2

Unit Measurement	1″	1¼″	2″	2½″	3″
Repeat section width	6″	9″	12″	15″	18″
Border width	2″	3″	4″	5″	6″

REPEAT SECTION PIECING

1.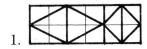

2.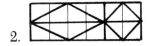

3.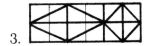

PIECES REQUIRED

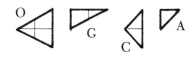

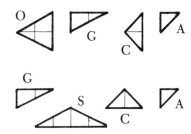

CORNER VARIATION

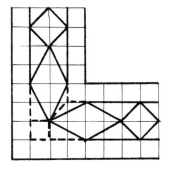

EXTRA PIECES REQUIRED

43

BORDER 31

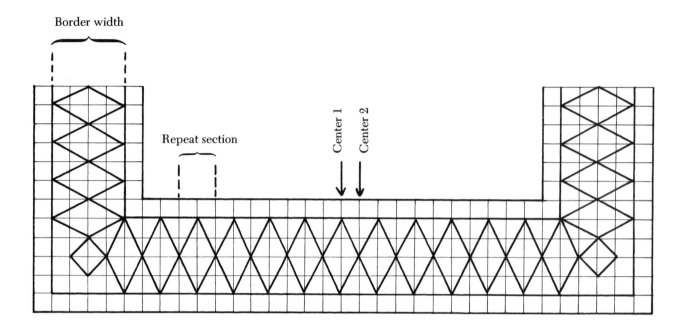

Border width

Repeat section

Center 1 Center 2

Unit Measurement	1″	1½″	2″	2½″	3″
Repeat section width	2″	3″	4″	5″	6″
Border width	4″	6″	8″	10″	12″

REPEAT SECTION PIECING	PIECES REQUIRED	CORNER PIECING	EXTRA PIECES REQUIRED

1.

 G

A
U
I

2.

 G S

3.

 G O

BORDER 32

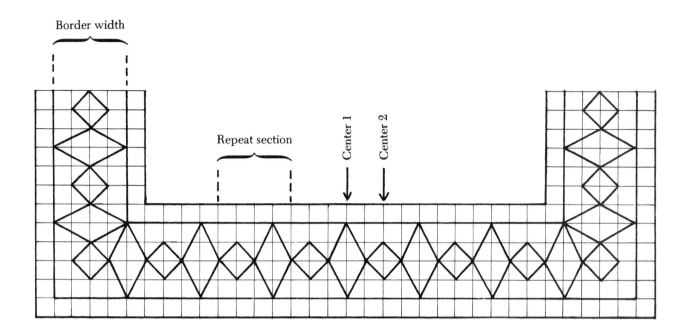

Unit Measurement	1″	1½″	2″	2½″	3″
Repeat section width	4″	6″	8″	10″	12″
Border width	4″	6″	8″	10″	12″

REPEAT SECTION PIECING   **PIECES REQUIRED**   **CORNER PIECING**   **EXTRA PIECES REQUIRED**

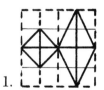

1.

2.

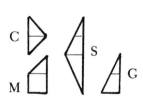

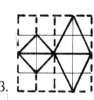

3.

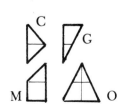

45

BORDER 33

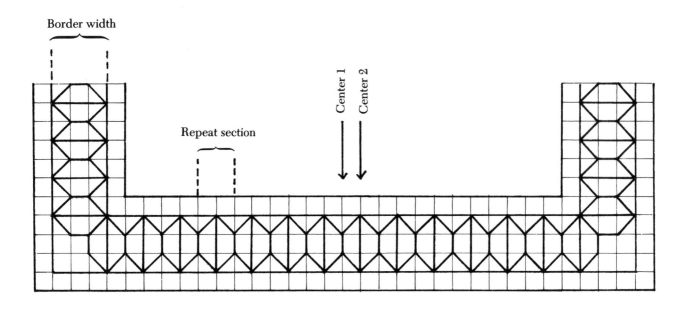

Border width

Repeat section

Center 1

Center 2

Unit Measurement	1″	1½″	2″	2½″	3″
Repeat section width	2″	3″	4″	5″	6″
Border width	3″	4½″	6″	7½″	9″

REPEAT SECTION PIECING

PIECES REQUIRED

A   R

CORNER PIECING

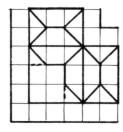

EXTRA PIECES REQUIRED

K

BORDER 34

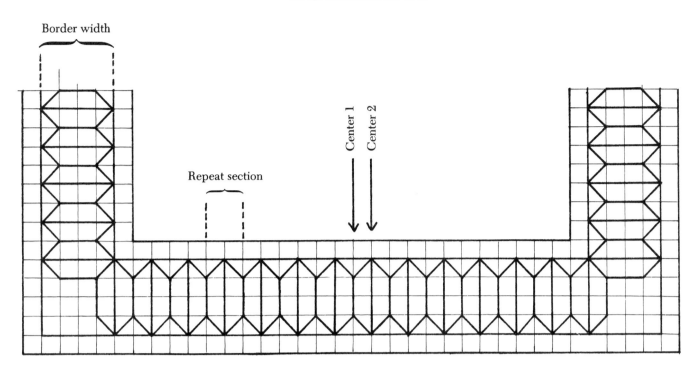

Border width

Repeat section

Center 1 Center 2

Unit Measurement	1″	1½″	2″	2½″	3″
Repeat section width	2″	3″	4″	5″	6″
Border width	4″	6″	8″	10″	12″

REPEAT SECTION PIECING

PIECES REQUIRED

T

A

CORNER PIECING

EXTRA PIECES REQUIRED

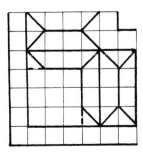

Block,
three units
square

BORDER 35

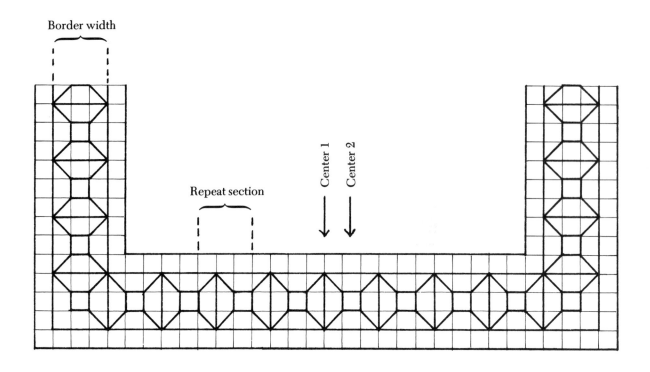

Unit Measurement	1″	1½″	2″	2½″	3″
Repeat section width	3″	4½″	6″	7½″	9″
Border width	3″	4½″	6″	7½″	9″

REPEAT SECTION PIECING

PIECES REQUIRED

N   R   A

CORNER PIECING

EXTRA PIECES REQUIRED

M

BORDER 36

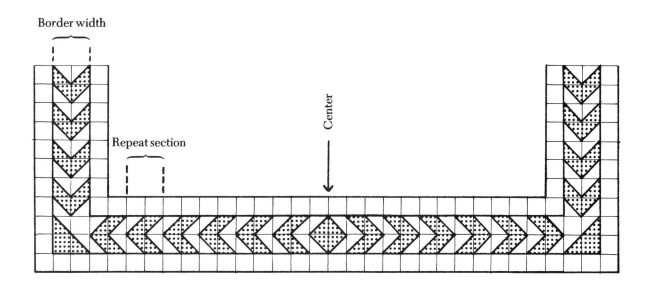

Unit Measurement	1″	1½″	2″	2½″	3″
Repeat section width	2″	3″	4″	5″	6″
Border width	2″	3″	4″	5″	6″

REPEAT SECTION
PIECING

PIECES REQUIRED

1.

A   C

2.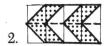

P

CORNER PIECING

EXTRA PIECES
REQUIRED

CORNER VARIATION

E

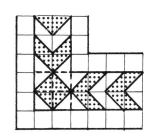

BORDER 37

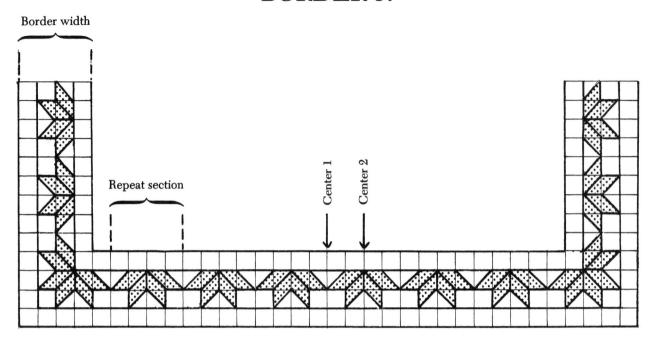

Border width

Repeat section

Center 1

Center 2

Unit Measurement	1″	1½″	2″	2½″	3″
Repeat section width	4″	6″	8″	10″	12″
Border width	2″	3″	4″	5″	6″

REPEAT SECTION PIECING

PIECES REQUIRED

A   P   N

CORNER PIECING

CORNER VARIATIONS

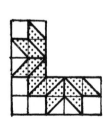
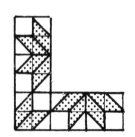
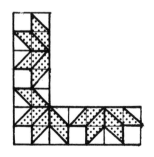

Variation 1

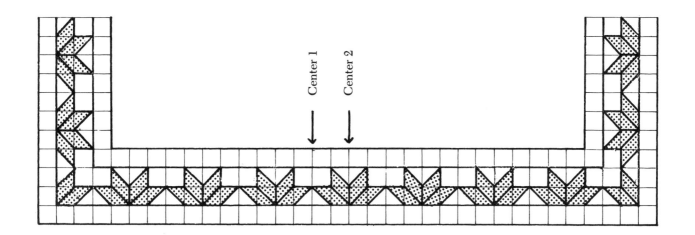

CORNER PIECING

CORNER VARIATIONS

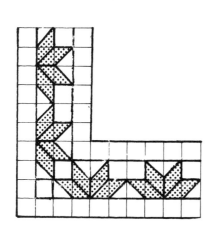

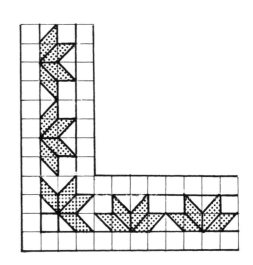

BORDER 38

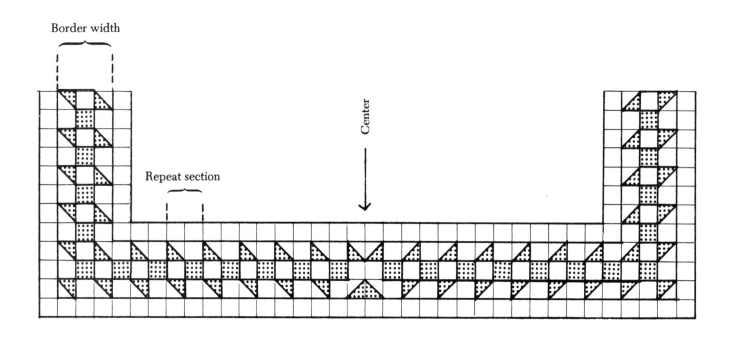

Unit Measurement	1″	1½″	2″	2½″	3″
Repeat section width	2″	3″	4″	5″	6″
Border width	3″	4½″	6″	7½″	9″

REPEAT SECTION PIECING

PIECES REQUIRED

N   A

CENTER PIECING

BORDER 39

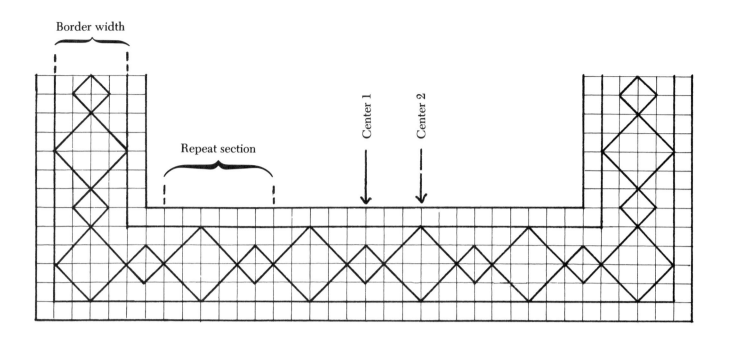

Unit Measurement	1″	1½″	2″	2½″	3″
Repeat section width	6″	9″	12″	15″	18″
Border width	4″	6″	8″	10″	12″

REPEAT SECTION PIECING

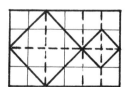

PIECES REQUIRED

E   A   M

CORNER VARIATION

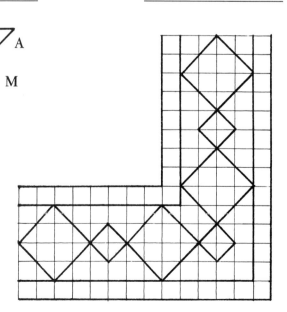

BORDER 40

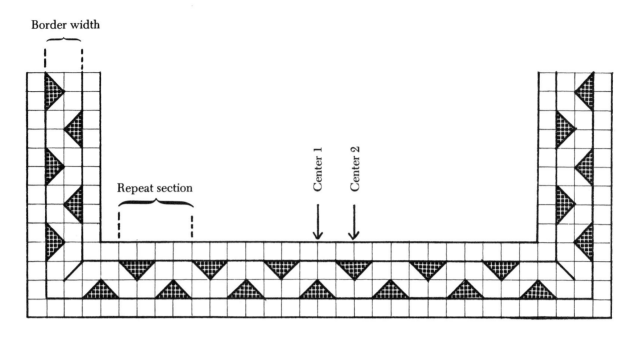

Unit Measurement	1″	1½″	2″	2½″	3″
Repeat section width	4″	6″	8″	10″	12″
Border width	2″	3″	4″	5″	6″

REPEAT SECTION
PIECING

PIECES REQUIRED

1. 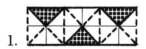

2. 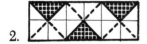   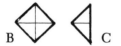

CORNER PIECING

1.

2.

54

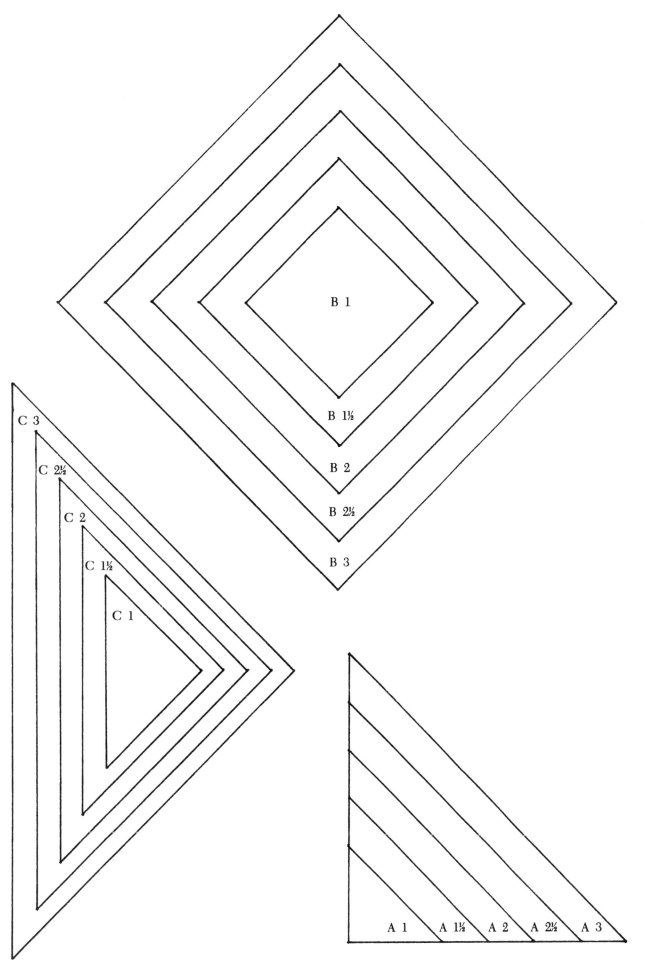

B 1

B 1½

B 2

B 2½

B 3

C 3

C 2½

C 2

C 1½

C 1

A 1 A 1½ A 2 A 2½ A 3

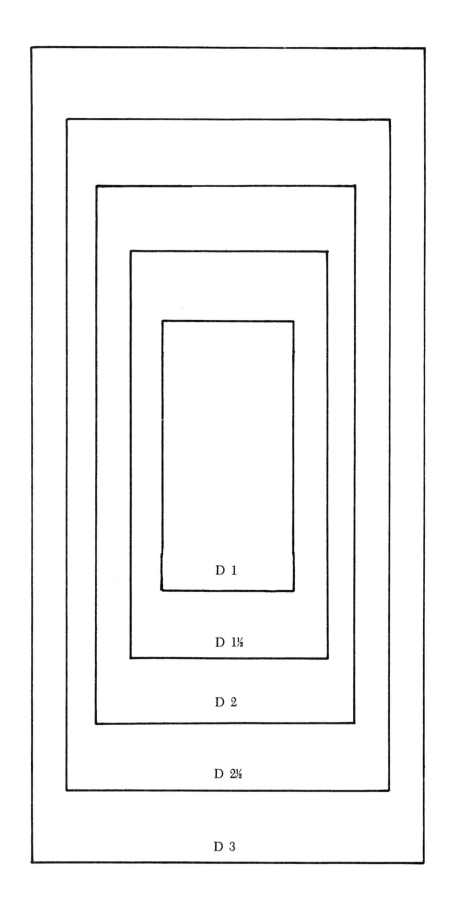

D 1

D 1½

D 2

D 2½

D 3

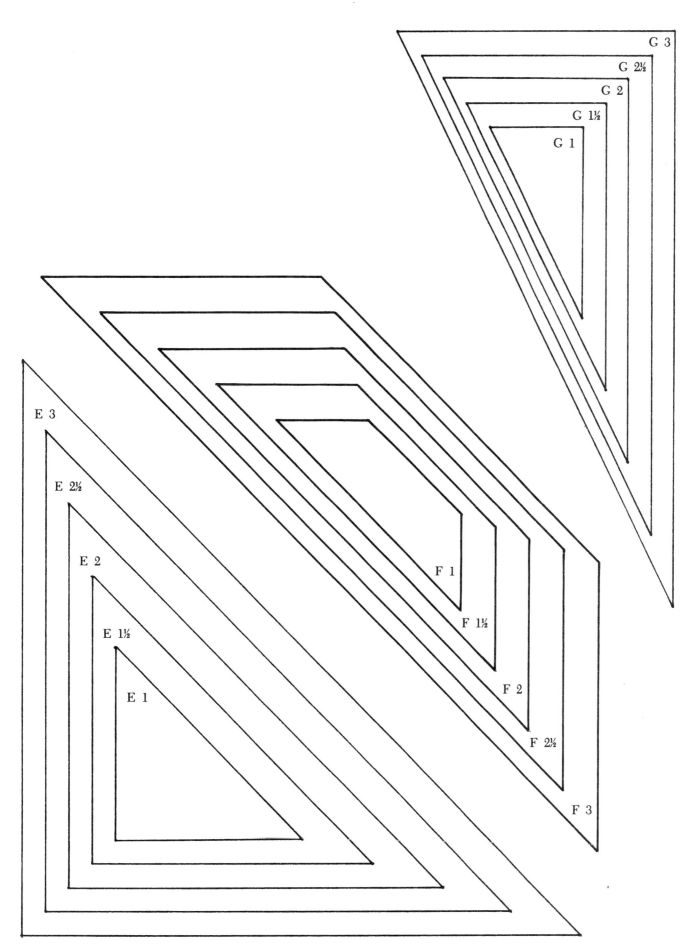

E 3

E 2½

E 2

E 1½

E 1

G 3

G 2½

G 2

G 1½

G 1

F 1

F 1½

F 2

F 2½

F 3

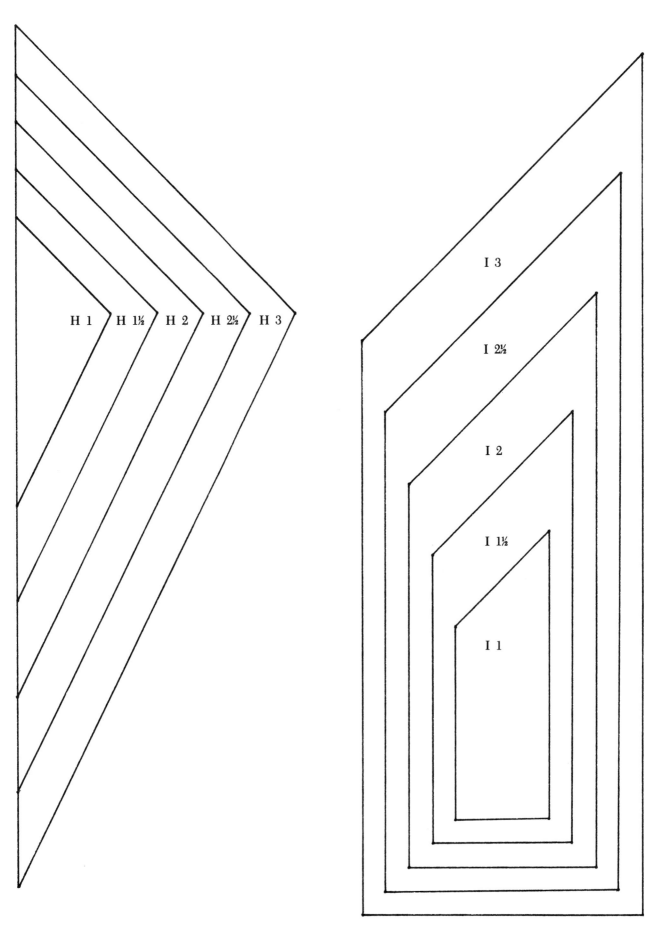

H 1 H 1½ H 2 H 2½ H 3

I 3

I 2½

I 2

I 1½

I 1

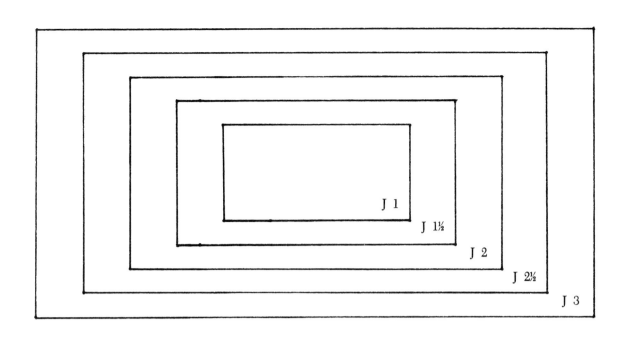

J 1
J 1½
J 2
J 2½
J 3

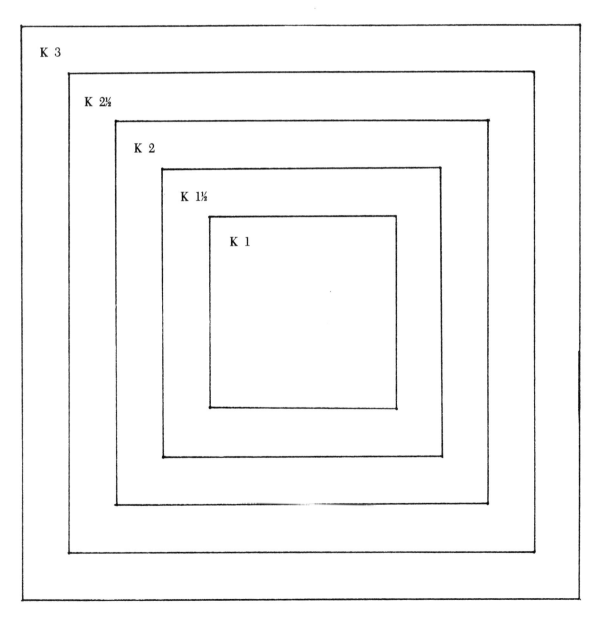

K 3
K 2½
K 2
K 1½
K 1

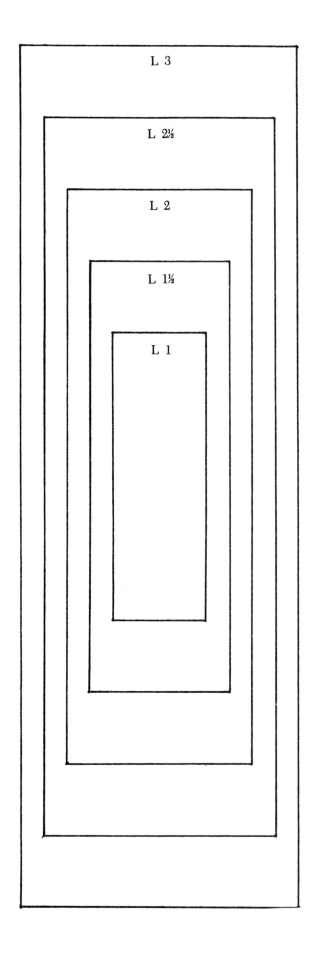

L 3

L 2½

L 2

L 1½

L 1

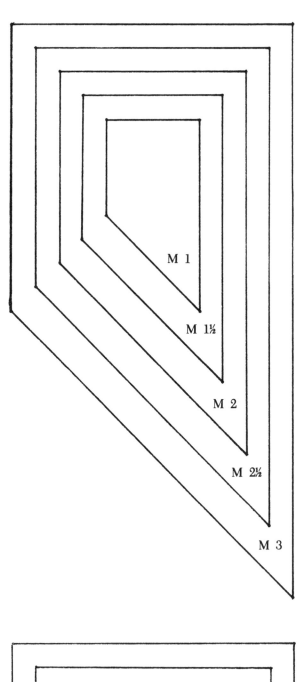

M 1

M 1½

M 2

M 2½

M 3

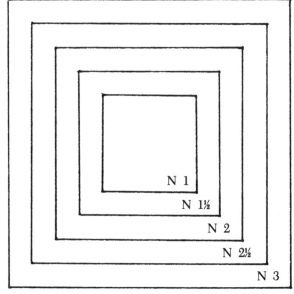

N 1

N 1½

N 2

N 2½

N 3

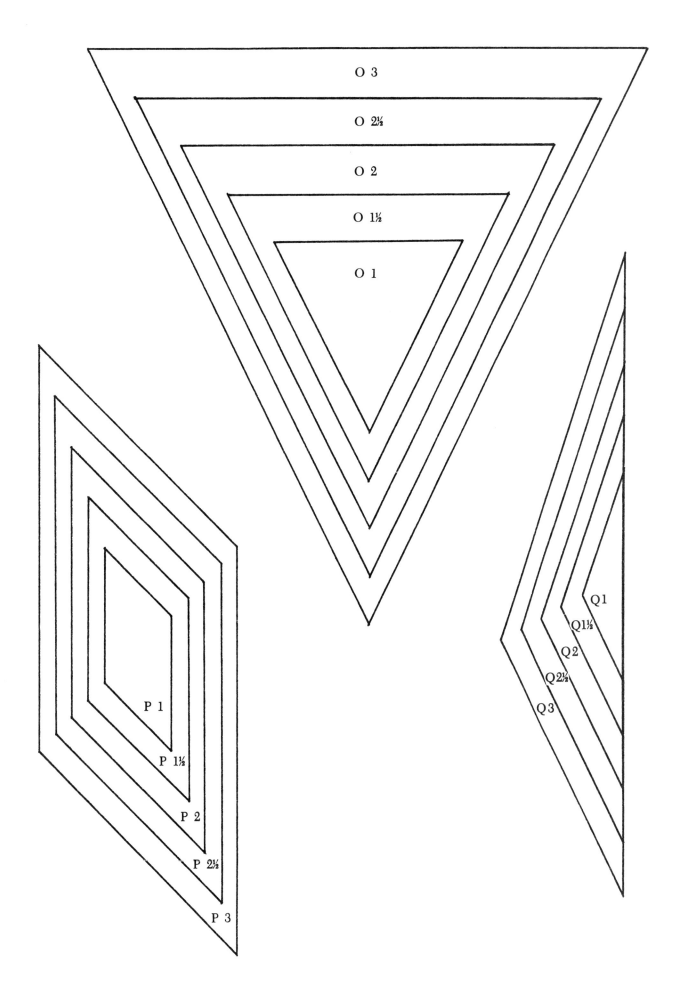

O 3

O 2½

O 2

O 1½

O 1

P 1

P 1½

P 2

P 2½

P 3

Q1

Q1½

Q2

Q2½

Q3

R 3

R 2½

R 2

R 1½

R 1

S 1

S 1½

S 2

S 2½

S 3

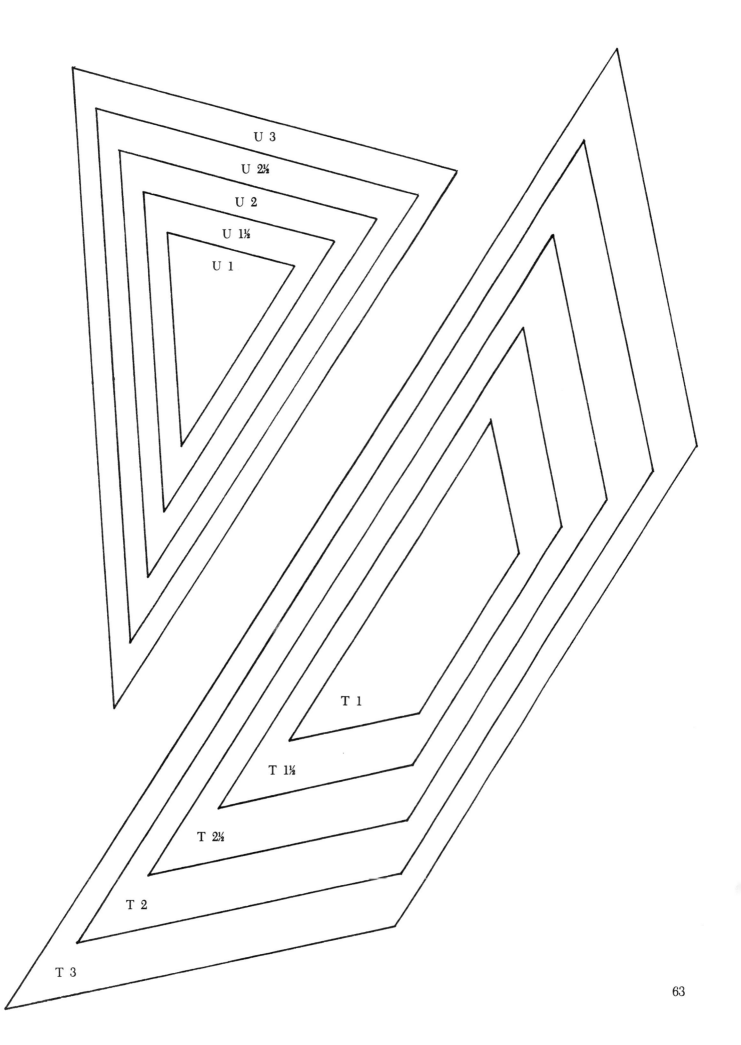

U 3

U 2½

U 2

U 1½

U 1

T 1

T 1½

T 2½

T 2

T 3

63

METRIC CONVERSION CHART

CONVERTING INCHES TO CENTIMETERS AND YARDS TO METERS

mm — millimeters   cm — centimeters   m — meters

INCHES INTO MILLIMETERS AND CENTIMETERS
(Slightly rounded off for convenience)

inches	mm		cm	inches	cm	inches	cm	inches	cm
⅛	3mm			5	12.5	21	53.5	38	96.5
¼	6mm			5½	14	22	56	39	99
⅜	10mm	or	1cm	6	15	23	58.5	40	101.5
½	13mm	or	1.3cm	7	18	24	61	41	104
⅝	15mm	or	1.5cm	8	20.5	25	63.5	42	106.5
¾	20mm	or	2cm	9	23	26	66	43	109
⅞	22mm	or	2.2cm	10	25.5	27	68.5	44	112
1	25mm	or	2.5cm	11	28	28	71	45	114.5
1¼	32mm	or	3.2cm	12	30.5	29	73.5	46	117
1½	38mm	or	3.8cm	13	33	30	76	47	119.5
1¾	45mm	or	4.5cm	14	35.5	31	79	48	122
2	50mm	or	5cm	15	38	32	81.5	49	124.5
2½	65mm	or	6.5cm	16	40.5	33	84	50	127
3	75mm	or	7.5cm	17	43	34	86.5		
3½	90mm	or	9cm	18	46	35	89		
4	100mm	or	10cm	19	48.5	36	91.5		
4½	115mm	or	11.5cm	20	51	37	94		

YARDS TO METERS
(Slightly rounded off for convenience)

yards	meters	yards	meters	yards	meters	yards	meters	yards	meters
⅛	0.15	2⅛	1.95	4⅛	3.80	6⅛	5.60	8⅛	7.45
¼	0.25	2¼	2.10	4¼	3.90	6¼	5.75	8¼	7.55
⅜	0.35	2⅜	2.20	4⅜	4.00	6⅜	5.85	8⅜	7.70
½	0.50	2½	2.30	4½	4.15	6½	5.95	8½	7.80
⅝	0.60	2⅝	2.40	4⅝	4.25	6⅝	6.10	8⅝	7.90
¾	0.70	2¾	2.55	4¾	4.35	6¾	6.20	8¾	8.00
⅞	0.80	2⅞	2.65	4⅞	4.50	6⅞	6.30	8⅞	8.15
1	0.95	3	2.75	5	4.60	7	6.40	9	8.25
1⅛	1.05	3⅛	2.90	5⅛	4.70	7⅛	6.55	9⅛	8.35
1¼	1.15	3¼	3.00	5¼	4.80	7¼	6.65	9¼	8.50
1⅜	1.30	3⅜	3.10	5⅜	4.95	7⅜	6.75	9⅜	8.60
1½	1.40	3½	3.20	5½	5.05	7½	6.90	9½	8.70
1⅝	1.50	3⅝	3.35	5⅝	5.15	7⅝	7.00	9⅝	8.80
1¾	1.60	3¾	3.45	5¾	5.30	7¾	7.10	9¾	8.95
1⅞	1.75	3⅞	3.55	5⅞	5.40	7⅞	7.20	9⅞	9.05
2	1.85	4	3.70	6	5.50	8	7.35	10	9.15

AVAILABLE FABRIC WIDTHS

25″	65cm	50″	127cm
27″	70cm	54″/56″	140cm
35″/36″	90cm	58″/60″	150cm
39″	100cm	68″/70″	175cm
44″/45″	115cm	72″	180cm
48″	122cm		

AVAILABLE ZIPPER LENGTHS

4″	10cm	10″	25cm	22″	55cm
5″	12cm	12″	30cm	24″	60cm
6″	15cm	14″	35cm	26″	65cm
7″	18cm	16″	40cm	28″	70cm
8″	20cm	18″	45cm	30″	75cm
9″	22cm	20″	50cm		